To Our Young Readers:

Belize is home to a rapidly disappearing jaguar population whose natural prey is also becoming increasingly scarce. Jaguars sometimes seek food such as sheep and cattle from nearby farms whose farmers view jaguars as a serious problem.

The latest entrant to the Turtle Pond Collection is a jaguar named Junior Buddy born at the Belize Zoo. With a mother too sick to care for him, Junior Buddy was raised by the zoo's staff. Word of the baby jaguar spread quickly. Now, though fully grown, Junior Buddy attracts thousands of people to visit him each year. He has become a symbol for the endangered jaguar.

Junior Buddy reminds us that the survival of every species is crucial to keep the world in balance. As global citizens and problem-solvers, we must find solutions together to preserve the only planet we have. It's important to keep the basic needs— food, water, shelter—of people balanced while protecting our endangered species.

With hope for all,
Craig, Juliana, and Isabella Hatkoff

With special thanks to Sharon Matola,
Director of the Belize Zoo, and her staff

Photo credits: Front and back cover, pages 6–17 © 2007 by Nancy and John Kennedy; pages 18, 20–29 © 2008 by Carol Farneti Foster; Pages 4–5, 19 © 2010 by the Belize Zoo.

Text copyright © 2010 by Turtle Pond Publications LLC

All rights reserved. Published by Scholastic Inc. SCHOLASTIC, CARTWHEEL BOOKS, and associated logos are trademarks and/or registered trademarks of Scholastic Inc. Lexile is a registered trademark of MetaMetrics, Inc.

ISBN 978-0-545-23096-4

10 9 8 7 6 5 4 3 2 1   10 11 12 13 14 15/0

Printed in the U.S.A. 40
First printing, September 2010

Junior Buddy
A Jaguar's Tale

Told by
JULIANA, ISABELLA, *and* CRAIG HATKOFF

Photos by John Kennedy and Carol Farneti Foster

Cartwheel
·B·O·O·K·S·®

SCHOLASTIC INC.

New York   Toronto   London   Auckland
Sydney   Mexico City   New Delhi   Hong Kong

In a jungle in Central America, there is a special place for animals. It is the Belize Zoo, and it is unlike any other zoo. All the animals here can be found in the tropical forests of Belize. Some of these animals are black howler monkeys, toucans, tapirs, and jaguars.

A young jaguar named Junior Buddy lives at the Belize Zoo. Junior Buddy's mother lived in the wild, but she was sick. She was too weak to catch her normal food, so she started hunting sheep. The farmers did not want to lose their sheep, so they set a trap and caught her. Once they trapped the jaguar, the farmers decided to call the Belize Zoo.

The zookeepers quickly drove a truck to the small town of Springfield and brought the jaguar back. The keepers named the jaguar Springfield, to thank the farmers for helping her. The vet said Springfield was very sick, and everyone worked to help her get better. Then one morning, the keepers had a surprise. Springfield had a cub!

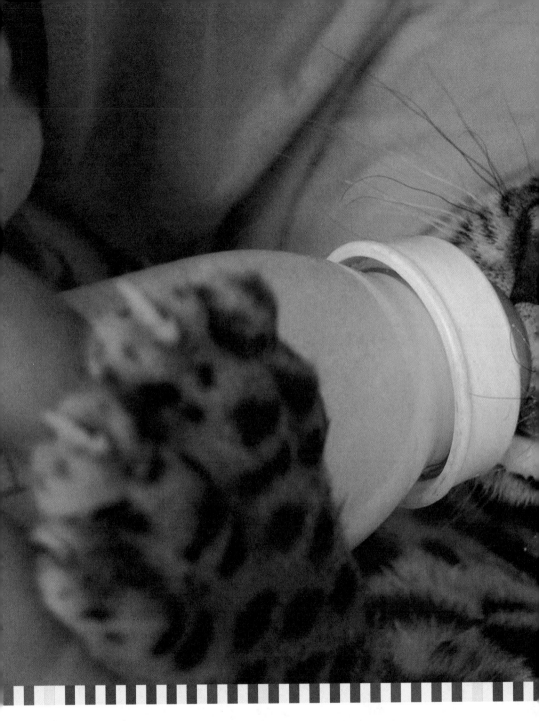

Springfield was still too weak to care for her baby. The keepers needed to help. They named the cub Junior Buddy.

The keepers tried to do the things a mother would do. First of all, they fed him. Junior Buddy was hungry!

Next he took swimming lessons!

Jaguars love to swim, but Junior Buddy wanted to take it slow. Even great cats do the doggy paddle.

Junior Buddy made friends with all the keepers.

They scratched his chin, and he nibbled their legs. Junior Buddy liked all the people who cared for him. They made him feel safe.

Junior Buddy started to grow stronger.

Before long, he was a curious and frisky cub.

Junior Buddy was always ready for fun.

He liked to play with sticks, balls, and seedpods.

It wasn't all fun and games. Junior Buddy had a lot to do. He had to figure out how to be a jaguar. For starters, he needed to

know how to climb trees. Learning had its ups and downs, but Junior Buddy was ready for any challenge.

For his first four months, Junior Buddy stayed in a special area at the back of the zoo.

When Junior Buddy was old enough, he moved to the main part of the zoo. This gave him more room to stretch out.

Junior Buddy's new space had a pool, a big new ball, logs for climbing, and lots of room to roam.

But he missed his friends. He paced
along the fence and yowled at night.

Junior Buddy was bigger now, and his teeth and claws were bigger, too! It was no longer safe for him to play in the same ways. The keepers came up with an idea. They built a cage inside Junior Buddy's space—it was a cage for people! Now his friends could pet him, scratch him behind the ears, and even sing to him.

The news about Junior Buddy began
to spread. A jaguar who likes people?
Visitors came to the Belize Zoo just
to see him.

The most amazing part was that his new friends could pet him, too! Junior Buddy loved the attention.

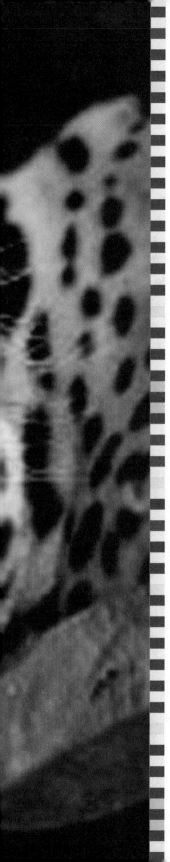

Before Junior Buddy, most people were scared of jaguars. Junior Buddy helped them see jaguars in a new way. After meeting him, kids decided to help save jaguars in the wild. They wrote letters asking other people to protect jaguars, too.

Junior Buddy has a safe home at the Belize Zoo because the keepers take care of him. But the jaguars in the wild are in danger. Each year, the jungles where they live and find their food are cut down for building projects, farms, and ranches. People have basic needs too. However, a loss of any species can throw Earth's life cycle off its delicate balance. We must seek solutions to help people as well as jaguars.

■

■ THE JAGUAR

The jaguar is the only great cat (of the Panthera genus) that lives in the Americas. The jaguars' recent range has been from the southwestern United States to northern Argentina. After the lion and the tiger, it is the largest of the cats. Jaguars are good swimmers and like to live near water. They eat a variety of foods, but prefer large prey such as deer, tapirs, and peccaries.

Jaguars have a spot pattern called a rosette, with a black dot in the center. While they look similar to leopards, leopards' spots do not have a center dot. The jaguar also has a sturdier frame, shorter legs, and a larger head. Most jaguars have black spots on a golden coat, but some have black spots on a black coat.

THE PROBLEM JAGUAR REHABILITATION PROGRAM

Jaguars who are sick or injured, or whose prey is disappearing, sometimes hunt sheep and cattle. Farmers will often shoot jaguars that come on their land in order to protect their own animals. To save the lives of jaguars, the Problem Jaguar Rehabilitation Program rescues "problem jaguars," jaguars that have killed farmers' sheep or cattle more than once. The program works with the animals that cannot be returned to the wild and helps them adapt to their new home. Some of these jaguars find homes in other zoos around the world. If more people can see these noble, beautiful animals, it improves the chances for saving them in the wild.

Springfield, Junior Buddy's mother, was rescued by the community of Springfield as a part of this program. She has fully recovered and now lives next to Junior Buddy at the Belize Zoo.

■ PANTHERA'S JAGUAR CORRIDOR INITIATIVE

Jaguars need to travel from place to place, both to find food and to meet up with other jaguars. It's good for animals from different areas to breed, so their cubs will have stronger bloodlines. Most jaguars like to live in remote areas, but building projects, roads, farms, and ranches have taken away a lot of their territory.

Panthera, an organization that works to protect great cats, is making a safe area for jaguars. It stretches from Mexico to Argentina and is called the Jaguar Corridor. It's not an actual road but a group of safe pathways that connect places where jaguars live. So far, thirteen countries are taking part. For it to work, ranchers need to keep their animals far from the corridor, so jaguars stay in the protected area. It will take a lot of effort on the part of many people, but it will help jaguars survive.